MW01641770

Hiawatha Asylum

poems by

Jennifer Soule

Finishing Line Press
Georgetown, Kentucky

Hiawatha Asylum

ISBN 978-1-62229-807-5 First Edition

ACKNOWLEDGMENTS

I wish to thank the following journals where these poems first appeared, some in slightly different variations:

"Goodwill." *Plainsongs* XXIV, 2(2004).
"Homeless at McDonald's." *South Dakota Magazine* May-June 2002.
"Morning Takes." *South Dakota Review* 43.1-2 (2005).
"Snow Geese." *South Dakota Journal of Medicine* 55.5 (2002).
"Hiawatha Asylum for Insane Indians." *South Dakota Review* 47, Number 2. Summer 2009.
"Finding Hiawatha." *Coal Hill Review* [online] 32:2013.
"Smoking Mr. V." *Sow's Ear.*
"Hotel Hot Springs." *Coal City Review* [forthcoming].
"deshabille." *Birmingham Poetry Review* (2008).
"Wind." *South Dakota Magazine* May 2002.
"Feral Peacocks." *The Briar Cliff Review* 26, 2014

Editor: Christen Kincaid

Cover Art: Brad Soule

Author Photo: Brad Soule

Cover Design: Elizabeth Maines

Printed in the USA on acid-free paper.
Order online: www.finishinglinepress.com
also available on amazon.com

Author inquiries and mail orders:
Finishing Line Press
P. O. Box 1626
Georgetown, Kentucky 40324
U. S. A.

Table of Contents

In gratitude to my mother Leone Kayl for her early sharing of a love of reading and poetry as well as her ongoing enthusiasm and encouragement of my writing.

I am ever grateful to my husband poet/partner Brad for his unwavering support.

This work is also dedicated to the memory of those women, men and children who lie buried at Hiawatha Asylum.

HIAWATHA ASYLUM FOR INSANE INDIANS

I. FINDING HIAWATHA

Highway 18 runs past the Canton grain elevators
to Hiawatha Golf Club where the restrooms
read: "Braves" and "Squaws."
Mid-fairway lies a graveyard—fenced—
sunken remains of 120 men and women who died
at Hiawatha Asylum for Insane Indians.
The city bought the old Asylum grounds
with stipulated "recreational use." No mention
of sacred ground on these soft Coteau des Prairies.

A faded prayer flag flutters in the wind.
Near the small burial plot a sign reads:
"Please do not play balls from the rough,"
A monument lists names of the dead:
Blue Sky, Long Time Owl Woman,
Yells at Night, Red Crow,
James Crow Lightning, Edith Standing Bear.
The golfers play through without a glance.

II. U.S. SENATE FLOOR PLEA OF RICHARD PETTIGREW (SD)

An effort to obtain Federal funds in 1899. A found poem.

It has been well established that the percentage
of insanity is greater among half-breeds
than among the full-blooded Indians.
This is explained by the theory
of cross-breeding, that has a tendency
to weaken the race.
For this reason it is confidently expected
by those who have made a study of these conditions
that the rate of insanity will greatly increase
as our civilization develops. The peculiar mental
afflictions of the Indians make it impractical
to treat them in connection with whites.
Association with their ancient enemy has,
it is said, a harrowing effect upon them.

Also it has been demonstrated by experience
that the various state asylums for the treatment
of the insane are not kindly disposed
toward receiving Indian patients.

III. HOW TO GET COMMITTED TO THE HIAWATHA ASYLUM FOR INSANE INDIANS

First, you must be Chippewa, Navajo,
Pawnee, Lakota, Crow or Winnebago.

Dance the Ghost Dance
to bring back the buffalo.

Have a seizure and fall down—
but the easiest way: anger an Indian agent.

Get in a loud argument with your wife's
brother because he said she sounded like a crow.

Talk to your dead ancestors about
what troubles you. Pray for their wisdom.

Believe you are White Buffalo Woman—
hold pipe ceremonies for days with no sleep.

Carry a congenital deformity
or become senile.

Tell your teacher you don't care
about Pilgrims and want to study Crazy Horse.

Refuse to let your children go
to the Carlisle Boarding School.

Conduct a healing ceremony
with special herbs for your mother.

Have a party with a group of cousins
and friends. Get rowdy, wake the Indian agent.

Reject Christianity,
refuse Western medicine.

Live on an Indian reservation
in the middle of nowhere.

Get drunk and lie down in fire.

IV. AUGUSTANA ACADEMY STUDENT WRITES HER FAMILY (SEPTEMBER 8, 1929)

I like the school, but I miss you.
Last week we went
to the Indian Insane Asylum
for a picnic. We shared lunches
with the patients. They seem sad—
like Grandpa was when Grandma died.
One older woman cried softy
the whole time. I think her name
is Blue Sky. I like the Indian names
because they sound like poems.
Blue Sky's long black hair looks like
a wave of first-plowed dirt. She wants
to go home to her people. I understand.
I bet she'd rather cook her own meals
and eat with family. Our food
is pretty good. Last night
we had pot roast, corn on the cob,
and apple pie. I know you are busy
with the harvest. There is a grain elevator
across the street and the pink corn dust
settles all over town like a winter sunset.

V. DR. SILK WRITES HOME (MARCH 20, 1929)

Dr. Samuel Silk, a psychiatrist from St. Elizabeth's Hospital in Washington, was dispatched to investigate problems at the Hiawatha Asylum for Insane Indians in Canton, SD.

The trip was long, the Appalachians
giving way to a vast unknown

of land where towns spring full blown from fields.
March is winter here: few signs
of spring. No cherry blossoms. In this place
the wind wails constantly, competes
with angry gods of mud and melting snow.
The Chinese Canton strikes one odd
where so many speak Norwegian,
celebrating Scandinavian feasts.
The grasses once were taller than these Nords.
This sea of green swallowed up some whole.
Ghosts of a buried prairie shimmer,
haunting the flat horizon.

VI. LONG TIME OWL WOMAN HAUNTS THE CANTON HOSPITAL

Last night I heard a clumsy bird
whirl in like a sick
stumbling buffalo. It coughed
and landed on the spit of cement.
A bad omen, this bird that swallows
the sick into its swollen belly,
flies straight up and leaves.
My people healed with help
from the natural world. Not machines
and surgery. I've seen strange things
while wandering the hospital halls: hurt
babies in plastic boxes crying and no one there.
I want to comfort them, but can't.
I couldn't comfort those little ones born
at the Asylum. I sang for them, but then
they were gone like the owl in the morning.
The night is my home. Sometimes now
I whistle to the dying.

VII. DR. SILK WRITES HOME (MARCH 21, 1929)

The problems are enormous already.
My days are long. We went between

two buildings of the hospital—the wind
blew snow straight in my face. Your long wool scarf
was welcome. Thank you. Conditions
are dubious. Patient with a tumor
on the brain was locked in solitude
so others could not see him. Another
secluded in a room to prevent fights.
Not necessary, I shall request his release.
A strait-jacketed boy on the cold floor,
retarded, chamber pot uncovered, full.
Another WWI vet shut away. A place
of padlocks and chamber pots. There are so many.
I feel as though I've fallen into a darker decade.

VIII. YELLS AT NIGHT

A Nurse's note

Last night his cries pierced my dreams.
I checked, but could not penetrate the pain.
Who bestowed this name
without a melody or meaning, blaming him?
Many patients lose their given names
to ignorance of native tongues. Many,
committed for refusing to speak
our English language. The sounds last night
bore an ancient rhythm beating from the earth.
Perhaps he once performed the Ghost Dance
and dreams of buffalo and antelope
that return, the men who corralled him
disappearing like some summer storm
blowing winds of disaster, then leaving prairie sun.

IX. DR. SILK WRITES HOME
MARCH 22, 1929

During my breakfast at the hotel
(which was pretty good with fresh eggs
and corn-fed bacon, crisp as October)
I noticed a cabinet with "souvenirs"
from the asylum for sale. A customer

exclaimed over the fine detail on a painted plate
from "a crazy Indian." I bristled as the clerk
laughed and rang up the sale. The city touts
the asylum as an attraction, "a spectacular treat
to complete a shopping day in Canton."
Patients string beads into necklaces, handbags,
and weave baskets of strong prairie grasses. Blue Sky
handed me one the other day, smiled. A gift that
would be rude to refuse. You will enjoy it.
Quill chokers quiver with colors of this lonely
landscape. I see therapeutic value in creative activity,
but they do not reap the profits. The citizens
are pleased to have a federal facility that brings
good income to town. But I don't think
it will be here much longer. Findings
are not auspicious for continuation.
The patients do not receive half
the attention you give your African violets.

X. AUGUSTANA ACADEMY STUDENT WRITES HER FAMILY OCTOBER 4, 1929

Last night I heard five rings
on our dorm phone, signal
of an Asylum Indian escape.
I was studying late for a test
when it shrilled through
like a coyote's call. I'd run, too.
When we last visited the place
to sing hymns for the patients
I saw a girl who made me cry,
her hair matted. Dirty flowered dress
made for a woman, not a girl.
Only about ten, I think.
She didn't talk, her eyes beamed fear.
Can kids be crazy? How would I know
if I were crazy? I'd flee like deer
to the woods if I were her. Farm wives
would hide her in their barns, feed her.
No one is afraid of the Indians.

XI. DR. SILK WRITES HOME
MARCH 23, 1929

I talked with the laundress today.
I don't blame her for the filthy bedclothes
on the wards; black as dirt. She is kept busy
with curtains and notes; *we have a good many,*
and they are hard to iron. The patients lie
on bedspreads with shoes on she laments;
the wash is not as white as I'd like.
The heat is coal, the water hard.
She wants a permanent ironing board,
electric iron. I spoke with her of allegations
that Miss Fillious antagonizes the staff.
She reported *no difficulties of any kind with her.*
The problem here is not the head nurse.
Or laundry. Deeper than dirt;
lye soap will not wash it away.

XII. HIAWATHA VOLUNTEER

It makes me sad to visit
the Indians at the Insane Asylum.
Last week I gave Long Time Owl Woman
a bath and she just cried. She's getting frail.
Wants to go home to her people.
I can't blame her. I'd miss my family.
That Dr. H is not so nice. Why send
someone like him? He can't even drive
a tractor. I don't know what he does.
Never seen him in town. He's always
"having a bit to eat" at that nice home
they built for him. Lives alone.
No family. No wife. No kids.
Who'd live with him? The Indians
don't like him. There is nothing wrong
with them. Why Aunt Alma
has those spells during long winters
and her sister Ruth looks after her.
It's nothing bad. Just happens.

Like TB. People have broken parts.
You just live with it. Help out. No need
to throw them out or lock them away.
We've all got a few rusted, busted pieces.
We just patch them up the best we can
and go on. Bake a pie.

XIII. DR.SILK WRITES HOME
MARCH 24, 1929

A trying day and I would welcome
your wise womanly counsel.
Dr. Hummer has a solid
streak of misogyny running
down the back of his white coat.
He dislikes nurses. I had no desire
to enter this fracas, as I considered it
an internal matter. However,
during my interviews with staff I was
drawn into their quarrel.
There's raged a furious feud
between head nurse and Hummer
since she arrived. Miss F., a thirtyish woman
with a penchant for turquoise scarves,
exhibits neatness and professionalism.
Well-qualified, with good training,
she is energetic and shows a sympathetic attitude
toward patients. I believe you would
get on well with her. She enjoys
reading poetry, especially Gerald Manly Hopkins.
Dr. H. insists the kitchen and dining room staff,
along with laborers, furnish affidavits on her.
I suspect they may have thought this necessary
in order to keep their jobs. You will appreciate
one complaint by a young dining room girl
that Miss F. *carried on* at the dinner table,
telling stories and *associated with women*
in town who drank. The girl did not think
such was *lady-like*, nor was a previous
employee, who smoked cigarettes. She huffed

that she *was not brought up that way!*
But this is a diversion, my dear. There is great
sadness residing here under the cottonwoods.
These cold, clear nights I miss you.

XIV. DR. HUMMER DEFENDS HIMSELF

From 1908 to its closing in 1933, Dr. Hummer served as superintendent of the Hiawatha Asylum.

I did not choose this place.
Dr. White recommended me.
When young, I thought it would be
an adventure to go West. But it was
a mistake, this godforsaken field
of wild Indians—43 different tribes.
I can't get any histories; their tongue
is gibberish to me. Sure, many of the patients
are asymptomatic. But they can't go home
since they are "below normal," and must be
sterilized first. I have no means to do this.
The Asylum doesn't meet
standards, but what can I do?
I was not trained to treat Indians.

XV. NIGHT TRAIN

I recall when the Asylum closed. I was a girl.
We lived just east of Hiawatha then.
Perhaps it was November when the cold
hunkers down to stay. Outside, that night,
geese honking through clouds, I heard
the train whistle for the patients, their long ride
beckoning to St. Elizabeth's. They huddled
in blankets, waiting by big iron gates,
wind hurling around them. Empty building
hulked behind, that long dark winter solstice
shadowing all. Still, I thought, the city
may frighten them more. Here on the prairie
there's a certain quiet of sky and space.

XVI. DEATH AT HIAWATHA

The Lincoln County Court House recorded
one-hundred-eighty-nine Asylum deaths,

a deadly beginning
for seven children born there, on that list.

Average age at death was 42;
most common cause: tuberculosis.

Typical contemporary
non-Indian death: an octogenarian

Norwegian farmer killed by lightning plowing.
Best way to catch TB:

crowd people into poorly ventilated space
like German death camps.

Patients were not screened. Sputum exams
or chest x-rays could have saved many.
In South Dakota's surplus space,
fresh air they could not breathe.

XVII. DR. SILK WRITES HOME
MARCH 25, 1929

Today I had them apply restraints to me.
Only briefly attached with wristlets,
but patients endure entire nights like this.
I saw iron rings in Baltimore
at City Hospital where they chained
patients to walls. In Canton, the restraints
are kept by the Financial Clerk.
A *ward attendant* with no medical credentials
decides if a patient is to be restrained
and *the clerk* hands him the apparatus.
The practice stems from old wars and fears,

not illness. These patients are not criminals.
I am ready to be released and return home.

XVIII. A CANTON FARMER REMEMBERS

My dad and I worked at the old Asylum.
Piggery, dairy, corn cribs, horse barn, fields.
Just one farmer up there, no hands.
We did thrashing with Crazy Charlie—a good worker.
Hog butchered. Wasn't a very sanitary operation,
drainage bad. The women sat outside
in summer. Smiled and waved. Seemed real nice.
Big business in this corn and soybean county.
The town didn't want to lose that Fed money.
They shut down when we needed them the most—
Depression years. We don't talk of that place.
Kind of shameful. When they golf, they play around
that little cemetery with no markers.

XIX. LONG TIME OWL WOMAN HAUNTS HIAWATHA GOLF COURSE

I watch the locals
chase their balls in carts
around my burial ground.
I want to laugh,
lament: Hiawatha
Indian Insane
Asylum. Which we were not.
I was sent here to die away
from my people because
the Indian agent said
my dreams and visions were crazy.
My grandmother had them, too.
They help us see the unseen.
They are good. Not bad.
Fenced in death, in life
we could not be controlled.
My curse upon their scores!

Twisted be their swings!
Their balls, Gone! Laughing
I soar above the pines,
over these unmarked graves,
the broken doctors, bodies
left here by the fleeting
trickster on his path.

HOTEL HOT SPRINGS

They come from Denver, Kalispell,
Cheyenne, Grand Junction—all over the west—
to this small Black Hills town. Lakota winter
camping grounds—the Minnekahta—
veterans with nowhere else to go,
TB. Shell shock. No job, no wife, no home.
The river that never freezes claims mornings lost
in January and February mist.

A safe place to survive the blizzards howling
destitute, out of control, shelter sought,
the prairie frozen. Well-to-do and ill
arrived by rail to seek the healing waters
years ago, resorts run down become
the dark dives that line the river banks.

Veterans of WWI & II
checked into this old sanatorium
turned VA clinic—domiciliary
to stay for years forever. Domed red roof,
the wings hexagonal jut out toward town.

Later come more wars: Viet Nam,
Persian Gulf. Afghanistan. Iraq.
The wounded drifting and spilling
into cheap hotels—the Buffalo,
Frontier and Waterside last resorts
for bikers cowboys broken-down broken-up
men no one to love nowhere to go.

Winding into town between soft red
clay hills, the billboard shouts a welcome:
"Hot Springs—The Veteran's Town."

EVENING SHIFT

A different time—like story-time—
the patient quiet. Eyes closed, sighs.
I rub on medication-scented Dermassage
and for twenty minutes rub
the hospital away like chalk
from a blackboard full of care.

Lulled, relaxed, her muscles slack—
she talks about the accident.
Sometimes she cries, from the marrow,
the body speaking its own story.

SMOKING MR. V

The best part of his day was smoking.
Quadriplegic, blind, his home a VA
hospital bed, he needed a hand.
So twice a shift I held his cigarette,

into his lips, then out—a rhythm
easy enough for a Red Cross volunteer
who smoked him after school,
Tuesdays, Thursdays, 1962.

Since WWII, my dad smoked too.
Mr. V, who fought in WWI,
was older than my grandfather, and yet
he always greeted me, *Hi, beautiful.*

Gray shrunken shadow of a man,
his body concentrated at the core—
a giant head and heart worked overtime.
He listened to his bedside radio.

So, did you hear Paul Harvey?
Always something new to chat about
during the smoke. He had few visitors.
Not everybody called me beautiful.

SURPLUS BEANS

Like those Poor Laws of England
there is an Overseer of the Poor
in Jackson County. He decides
who deserves chicken or cheese.

Color and family figure in.
Butter rare as bricks of gold. The chickens
turn green in cans, but beans endure.
Extension department agents

with their mimeographed recipes
and strained smiles swarm back roads
determined to teach the poor 114 ways
to love the bean: lima, pinto, navy.

The struggle grinds Stella down
to dust too fine for making bread.

UPPER PENINSULA OF MICHIGAN

The locals taught me where to find morels—
those mysteries of dark earth places
that delight if you surprise them
hiding like kids in a mountain
of leaves; if you don't chose the poisonous
cousins by mistake. They showed me
how to dance dandelions and grapes
into wines, how to snowshoe out the second
story window and laugh about it.
What could I teach them?

GOODWILL

During the week
of Thanksgiving
a cabless semitruck
open, unattended
sulks in the City Parking lot
waiting to be filled.
Wind bays in drain spouts
ice congeals.
I drop off four
boxes of books
a text
on poverty in America
lands on top.
By Friday the truck,
is three quarters full—
clear blue plastic bags
contain worn tennis shoes
ragged striped towels
all sizes of closet discards
toys played out.
One beige appliance
in parts I can't identify.
I've heard that people sometimes
leave sheets soiled with semen
at homeless shelters.
The season of giving
now underway as Christmas
lights go up and the Salvation
Army sends its soldiers
into battle armed with bells.

HOMELESS AT McDONALD'S

A mother and grown daughter live quietly
in a blue Chevy van parked at McDonald's
at 41st and Minnesota.
Rusted van, a window duct-taped shut,
packed to the roof with boxes, blankets, lamps.
The mother limps on bandaged foot, balances
coffee, her daughter shuffling behind
with Egg McMuffins and condiments.
Here they eat and use the restroom
near the brightly colored kiddies' playground.
Homeless women aren't in ads or jingles.
Management doesn't police the parking lot.
The staff can picture being in that car—
knows everyone can't live in comfortable
homes too busy to cook healthy meals
with soccer, dance, piano, basketball.
McDonald's meals are happy ones with toys.
These women live here, hiding furtively
a movement in the dumpster's neon shadow—
homeless incorporate beneath
the golden arches of America.

SEEING MYSELF

At the mall I see another woman
wearing the candy cane sweater
I donated to Hannah's House.

Here is a woman, also small,
smiling at me, a stranger.
An odd feeling—
like seeing myself
walk into a mirror,
abracadabraed into

a different race, limping,
herding three kids.
Approaching from the other side
of some invisible line
that any woman
might be pushed across.

LIFE UPSTAIRS

She avoided eye contact and walked head down
as if to wear a sign: *Don't look.*
Don't talk to me or I'll be dead.
Her jailer husband—Green Beret—
attacked by night. The fights began
in their kitchen over our bedroom
and ended in their bedroom over
our kitchen. The bruises unseen.
She rarely moved her arms, was never
alone, nor answered the door
when he was gone. The women's shelter
was right next door. I volunteered there.
I knew if I intervened she might be
killed. She would have to escape
on her own, hide far away.
When I moved she was still alive.

FERAL PEACOCKS

One day the peacocks just arrived:
escaped, no doubt, from somewhere near.
They roosted in tall sycamores
beside the creek among the sheep
and close to the birdfeeder.
Needs all met, free of human schedules,
they entertained us. Male displays
with rattling feathers amused
through several reruns. But even
casual strutting (blue green-tails folded,
eyes closed) enchanted us—
especially in winter. Wild and tame
they settled in with icicles hung from them—
no snow birds these tough dudes.
They shrilled a human cry: "Help! Help!"
on eerie nights. It left you wondering.
Flannery O'Connor kept them as pets
on that Georgia farm among her feral souls.

SNOW GEESE

At dusk a shadow line
moves in the northern sky.
Monochromatic November
brightens, fills with snow geese.

Wings tipped black on luminous white,
they soar above snow dusted fallow fields
honking their way down the valley
in graceful floppy heart-stopping V's.

Southbound toward the Gulf of Mexico,
at sixty miles an hour with the wind
they follow the Big Sioux River
to feeding stops on yet unfrozen water.

The summer breeding marshes
will wait their return in springtime,
cycles of birth and death,
from Gulf to tundra waste and back again.

The line of geese is fading in the south.
A landscape, in black and white, lies harvested,
barren, as Arctic air roars in tonight
claiming the Great Plains for an ancient grief.

MORNING TAKES

Groggy, morning wakes
under a prairie canopy. Crows
caw at false light—half-hearted
in cool March air, dense fog,
landscape a seascape.
Pheasants desperate for food
run in frozen cornfields.
We make love at first light.
Bodies sensing spring
wake early—eager, wilder
creatures needing to mate.
Morning geese fly overhead.
Coyote howls behind a hill.
Animals are on the prowl.

deshabille

Once during a job interview
I was asked to remove my clothes.
Good Catholic Mount Marty College
reluctantly served figure drawing
on the side in their Christian curriculum.

The professor knew anyone too timid
to disrobe would not show up
and model for students. I stepped out
of my dress carefully chosen for a good
impression. All he needed
was "well-proportioned" and willing to stand
three hours next to a chair.

I got ten minute breaks. And in my chenille
robe I could even smoke. But students could not talk
to the loose woman. Good Catholic girls
kept their bodies under wrap and boys
did not entertain venial thoughts.
The nuns preferred everyone clothed
(like the Virgin Mary) but the professor
insisted on a human figure nude.

The job paid better than waitressing.
I could purchase my student ticket
to Europe, where nude was art.

WIND

Motorcycling in South Dakota
you become wind
on the prairie, queen of green
and gold and blue.
Flying down roads, you are
cornstalks dancing to exhaustion,
like the woman in red shoes.
Grasses bowing to wind's power.
So do we willingly submit
and on curves,
commit to another plain
for the ride's duration
wide open as the sky.

BENITA'S PHOTO

At 14th and Constitution
between the FBI and Smithsonian—
in February slush and valentines

the photography professor focuses
her 35 millimeter black and white eye.
The woman subject sleeps, snores

on a grate with steam
shrouding her stillness
Cars and walkers, urban glazed

by policy and lawmaking pass
her beauty. Hands of a Michelangelo
gnarled in prayer, captured in light.

Her photo hangs next to our front door.
Here people pause on leaving,
beckoned by the hands.

Jennifer Soule's poems have appeared in *South Dakota Review, The Sow's Ear Poetry Review* and *Modern Haiku,* among others including various anthologies. She has been a community organizer, clinical social worker and professor in various parts of the country. A South Dakota native, she recently returned there to Sioux Falls (hometown) with her husband Brad. As a professor emeritus (social work) with an MFA in creative writing, she now has time to combine her varied interests and devote more time to writing.

Her passion for place and love of language were well nurtured in South Dakota. She majored in English and sociology at USD then lit out for the territory of social change: during the sixties. She remained an inhabitant of the border world of words and activism and her career in social work satisfied these twin passions.

South Dakota reflects extremes of beauty and space. This is evident in such disparate areas as weather and history and well exemplified by the anguish of the bi-cultural conflicts of native Americans and pioneer farmers. The Hiawatha Asylum for Insane Indians (the actual historical institution) embodies these extremes. This led her to some extensive research and "poetry of witness" on that large canvas where poetry and life intersect.